The Babysitter's Backpack

Everything You Need to Be a **SAFE, SMART,** and **SKILLED BABYSITTER**

by Rebecca Rissman and Melissa Higgins

capstone
young readers

Table of Contents

Page 11

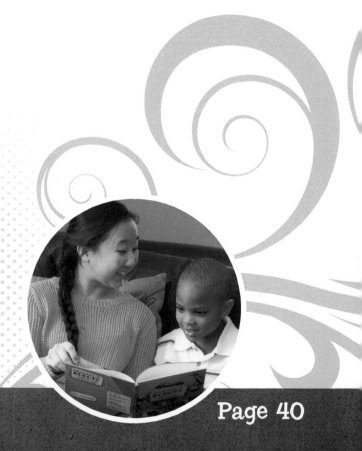

Page 40

Become a Great Babysitter

Your neighbor has a newborn you'd love to babysit. A family friend has two preschoolers and needs a babysitter. Your parents ask you to watch your little brother for a few hours. Before you say yes to any babysitting job, be sure you're ready for the responsibility that comes with it.

Before you begin babysitting, be sure you know the basics, including ...

- ❑ what qualities make a great babysitter
- ❑ basic child-care skills
- ❑ how to deal with behavioral issues
- ❑ basic first-aid skills
- ❑ how to keep kids safe
- ❑ how to manage your babysitting business
- ❑ how to keep kids entertained and have fun while you're babysitting

Sound like a lot? Don't sweat it. Take the time to learn important skills, such as how to hold a baby, what to do if a stranger comes to the door, and how to create a treasure hunt that will keep any 5-year-old entertained. With the right training, you'll be prepared for any babysitting job and know how to confidently handle any situation.

What Should You Do? quiz questions throughout will help you know if you're ready to be a great babysitter. You can look up the answers on page 122.

You're IN CHARGE

Basic Rules

Every

BABYSITTER

Needs to Know

Being a Responsible Leader

Babysitting is a fun and rewarding job, but it first requires responsibility and preparation. You may want to jump on the opportunity to start caring for children. First begin by learning about the skills and qualities you need to possess.

A responsible and prepared babysitter always knows:

- babysitting basics, such as feeding, diapering, and bathing
- the backgrounds of each child, such as health issues and food allergies, and how to handle them
- how to get in touch with the child's parents or guardians
- where emergency supplies, such as fire extinguishers and flashlights, are located
- the house rules and parents' expectations for you and their children
- simple first aid and when and where to call for help in an emergency
- to keep her full attention on the children and never leave children unattended

The more prepared you are, the more you'll be able to relax. You'll be able to have more fun with the children you're babysitting.

Qualities of a Great Babysitter

Leadership is one of the most important qualities of a great babysitter. Children need to understand you're in charge. When you're an effective leader, you build trust and earn the respect of both children and their parents.

Role modeling: Demonstrate the behavior you want from the children you babysit. If you want them to have a good attitude, always smile and show enthusiasm.

Respect: Respect your employer and the children in your care. Follow all household rules and routines. It also means respecting people as individuals, even if they are different from you.

Communication: When talking with children, use words and sentences they can understand. Show you're listening by sitting or kneeling so you are at eye level with the child.

Making decisions and taking action: Being in charge sometimes means making fast decisions and taking action. Watch for situations that might need your help. Ask yourself exactly what the problem is and what would be the best solution.

Caring: Good babysitters enjoy being around and taking care of children. Show you care by being friendly. But don't try to be "cool" and let the children do whatever they want. Children behave best with structure and limits.

Getting Started

You think you have all the right qualities to be a great babysitter. Before you start looking for a job, make sure you have the following points covered.

Get educated. Take babysitting classes and first-aid training.

Get your parents' approval. Know their rules and expectations for when, how often, and who you babysit.

Know your limits. Does caring for a newborn or a child with special needs make you nervous? What ages are you comfortable babysitting? Don't take a job that's not a good fit. Will babysitting conflict with your schoolwork or after school activities? Know how often you feel comfortable babysitting.

Find clients. Spread the word through family, friends, and neighbors that you're interested in babysitting.

Interview the family. When a new family asks you to babysit, you may want to jump at the opportunity. An interview lets you and the family figure out if you're a good match. Take a trusted adult or older sibling with you if you're going to meet a new family.

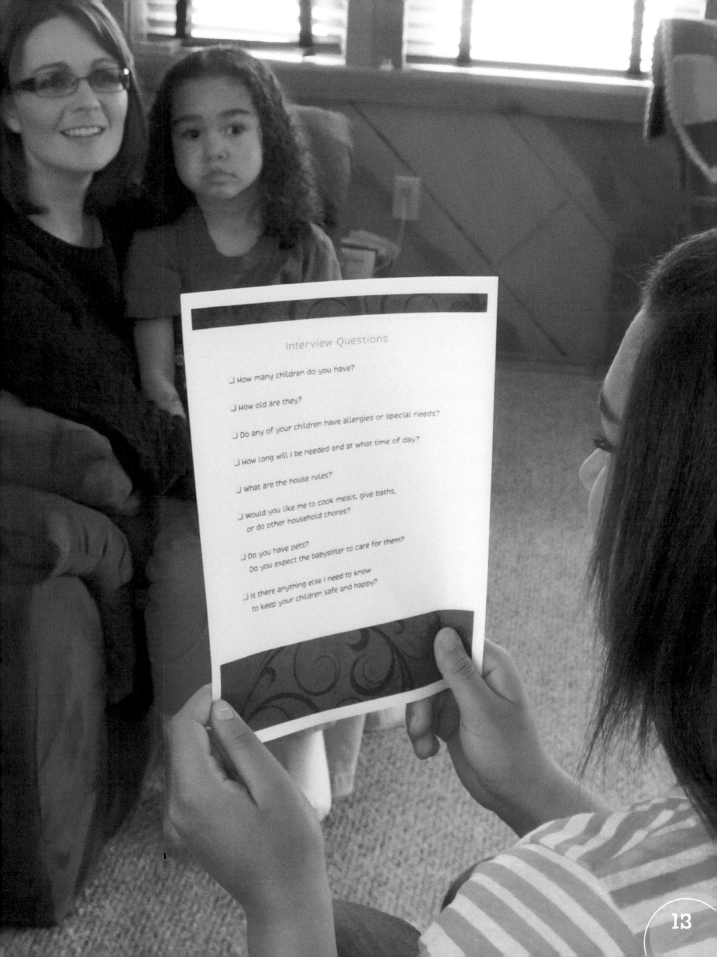

Interview Questions

❑ How many children do you have?

❑ How old are they?

❑ Do any of your children have allergies or special needs?

❑ How long will I be needed and at what time of day?

❑ What are the house rules?

❑ Would you like me to cook meals, give baths,
   or do other household chores?

❑ Do you have pets?
   Do you expect the babysitter to care for them?

❑ Is there anything else I need to know
   to keep your children safe and happy?

Child Care Basics: Safety and Routines

Safety is always your first priority when babysitting. Pay attention to what's happening around you and use your common sense. Stick to the rules and routines you have discussed with parents.

Safety

Before you perform any kind of child care, make sure you understand and can perform basic emergency procedures. Take a basic first-aid class. Know when and whom to call in an emergency.

Be Aware of Your Surroundings

Remember the key rules in babysitting. Pay attention and never leave children alone! Be aware of what's going on around you. Are there toys scattered around that a child could trip on? Are there small objects nearby that a toddler could choke on? Paying attention to these things will keep kids safe and happy.

What Should You Do?

A friend invites you to a sleepover for her birthday, but you already promised your neighbor you would babysit. You should ...

A Get your brother to babysit for you.

B Cancel the babysitting job. The neighbor will understand once you explain.

C Decline the sleepover invitation and go to your babysitting job.

D Do neither. Making tough decisions is stressful!

Know the Routines and Rules

Children are happiest when they follow their normal routines. Discuss children's routines and preferences with parents at the beginning of each job. You should know:

- What meals or snacks should children have? What foods are OK to eat?
- How much TV or electronics time is allowed? At what times?
- What TV shows are children allowed to watch? What video games are they allowed to play?
- What other activities are OK?
- Do the children need baths? What are the instructions for this?
- When is bedtime? What is the children's bedtime routine?

A parent is likely to write down some of the things you need to know while you're babysitting. It might look something like this.

We will be at the Johnsons until 10:30 p.m.
and will be home by 11:00 p.m.
The Johnsons' home phone is 555-8793
or call my cell at 601-555-0511.

The kids have had dinner.
They can have apples or microwave popcorn for a snack
but not too close to bedtime.

No TV after 8:00 p.m.
and absolutely no video games after 7:30 p.m.

Bedtime is 8:30 p.m. but no later than 9:00 p.m.
Their pajamas are on their beds.
Make sure they brush their teeth.

Please give Sanya her medication.
The bottle is on her dresser.
One teaspoon before bed.

In an emergency, our address is 1072 Elm Street.
If you can't reach us call Grandma Sally at 702-555-4489.

Caring for Infants and Toddlers

Dirty diapers. Thrown food. Keeping up with a 2-year-old. Caring for infants and toddlers can be messy and hectic. But it can also be fun when you're prepared and know what to expect.

Picking Up and Holding

Keep in mind that some children like to be held and others don't. Ask parents if their infant or toddler likes to be held. Respect each child's preference.

Infants: When holding an infant under 6 months old, always support the head, neck, and back. The child will feel more secure if you hold him close to your body.

Toddlers: Toddlers can be heavy. Make sure you're strong enough to give the child full support. Bend your knees and lift the child under the arms. Support the child with one arm under the bottom and your other arm supporting the back.

Sleep

Infants and toddlers do not always go to sleep easily and may cry. Ask parents in advance about their child's bedtime routine. Ask what to do when a child cries or has trouble falling asleep.

Sleep Safety Tips

Don't forget these safety tips when putting an infant or toddler to sleep in a crib.

❏ Be sure to remove any objects from an infant's crib, including pillows, stuffed animals, or other toys.

❏ Lay an infant face up on her back, unless a parent instructs you to lay the infant on her side. (In this case, have the parent show you exactly how to position her.)

❏ If the parents want you to cover their child with a blanket, tuck the bottom end of the blanket under the crib mattress. Then bring the blanket up to cover the child up to her chest.

Feeding

If you are asked to feed or prepare a meal for an infant or toddler, here are a few things to remember.

Bottle Feeding: Heat the bottle by holding it under warm running water. Never warm a baby's bottle in a microwave. Make sure it's not too hot by shaking a drop onto your wrist. Hold the baby so her head is supported and higher than the rest of her body. Tip the bottle so the nipple is always full of liquid. The baby will arch her back or push the nipple out of her mouth when she needs a break or is finished. Wait a few minutes, then touch the nipple to her lips to see if she wants more. Don't force a baby to eat more than she wants. After feeding, put a cloth over your shoulder. Hold the baby against your shoulder. Gently but firmly pat the infant's back until you hear a burp.

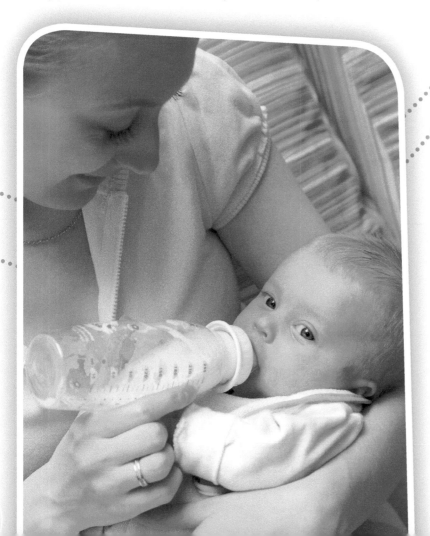

Spoon Feeding: Sit the baby in a highchair and fasten the safety straps. Put a little food on a baby spoon. Hold the spoon near the baby's mouth, and wait for the child to open his mouth. Put the food toward the middle of the baby's mouth. It's OK if he spits it out. Don't force him to eat.

Feeding Toddlers: Toddlers will likely use their fingers to eat. Be sure food is cut into very small pieces. Make sure the child sits while eating. Never leave a toddler alone when eating.

Diapering and Toileting

Infants frequently need their diapers changed. Always change a diaper if it's wet or dirty. Check diapers before and after nap time and feeding.

When changing a diaper, first gather all the supplies. These include a clean diaper, wipes, and diaper cream, if used. Place the supplies within reach of the changing area. Lie the baby on a changing table or flat surface. Use a safety restraint if there is one. Keep one hand on the baby. Do not leave the baby unattended. Remove the dirty diaper. Holding the baby's ankles, lift his hips and wipe thoroughly from front to back. Use diaper cream if parents have instructed you to. Properly dispose of the dirty diaper and wash your hands.

Toddlers who have recently learned to use the toilet may need your help in the bathroom. Ask parents what help the child will need. Know what words the toddler says when she needs to use the toilet. Wash the child's hands and your hands after helping a child use the toilet.

What Should You Do?

You're changing a 2-year-old's diaper and there's a knock at the front door. You should:

A Jump up and answer it. It might be important!

B Stay with the child and do not answer the door.

C Ask the 2-year-old's brother to answer the door.

D Quickly run to a window and see who it is.

23

Caring for Preschoolers and School-Age Children

Older children are more independent than infants and toddlers, but they still need your undivided attention. Stay near and watch children carefully. Provide help when they need it, and enjoy your time together.

Feeding

Preschoolers and school-age children vary in the foods they like and how much they eat. Start with small portions. Younger children are often messy eaters. Don't force a child to eat. A lack of interest in food is normal at this age. Preschoolers and school-age children can help with simple meal preparation. Have them help wash fruits and vegetables, put toppings on pizza, or set the table.

Toileting

Some preschoolers may still need help going to the bathroom. A parent will let you know how to handle this.

Sleep

Switch from lively to calming activities about 30 minutes before bedtime. Turn off the TV or computer. Play a quiet game or read bedtime stories. Let the child know about 15 minutes beforehand that bedtime is near. Make sure you follow the child's normal bedtime routine.

Bathing

Babysitters should not give baths to infants. If toddlers or older children need to be bathed, discuss bath-time routine with parents.

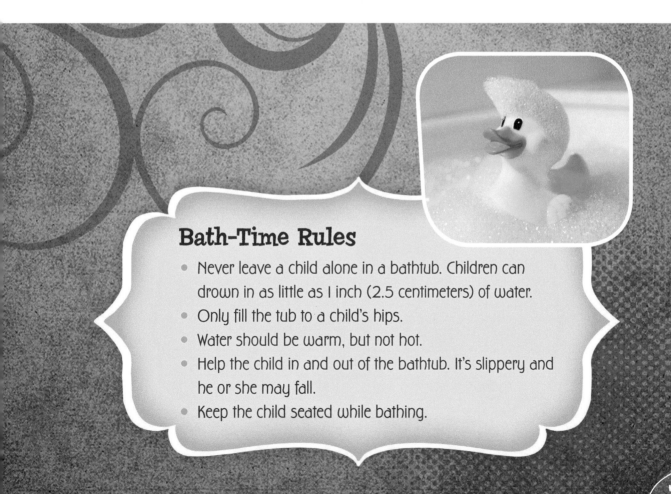

Bath-Time Rules

- Never leave a child alone in a bathtub. Children can drown in as little as 1 inch (2.5 centimeters) of water.
- Only fill the tub to a child's hips.
- Water should be warm, but not hot.
- Help the child in and out of the bathtub. It's slippery and he or she may fall.
- Keep the child seated while bathing.

Behavior Basics

There are many reasons children misbehave. A sibling is jealous of his brother or sister. A toddler is hungry, tired, or frustrated. A child wants attention or is bored. Great babysitters know how to deal with behavior problems when they arise or prevent them before they begin.

Encouraging Positive Behavior

A good way to keep behavior flare-ups from ever starting is to encourage positive behavior. Here are a few suggestions:

- Let children know when they've done a good job, such as when they put away their toys or go to bed on time. "Thanks for helping to put the blocks away. Putting toys away is easy when we work together."
- Set reasonable limits and let children know your expectations up front. "We're going to be together until your parents come home. We'll follow the same rules that you use every day."
- Don't favor one child over another.
- Be flexible. Don't force a child to take part in an activity if she doesn't want to play.
- Give advance notice when it's time to change from one activity to another, such as bedtime.
- Give children choices. "Do you want to play a game inside or outside?" If a child wants a soft drink but is not allowed, ask, "Do you want milk or water?"
- Smile and keep a good attitude. Have fun!

Correcting Misbehavior

Correcting misbehavior is one of the most challenging tasks you'll face when babysitting. Discuss with parents in advance how they handle problematic behavior. It's important to stay positive. Let the child know you're unhappy with the behavior, not the child.

You have three choices when faced with misbehavior.

- **Do nothing.** This is a good choice if a child is acting out for attention and not in danger of hurting himself or others.
- Most behavior problems are solved when you **say something.** In a calm voice, explain to the child why her behavior is not acceptable.
- There are times when you need to **use physical action** to control behavior. For example, if a child is about to throw a toy at his baby brother, take the toy away.

Remember!

It is never OK to shake, hit, or verbally insult a child. This is abuse. Shaking a child can cause brain damage and even death. No matter how frustrated you feel, stay calm and don't lose your cool. Take a deep breath. Think about the best way to handle the situation.

What Should You Do?

A 5-year-old refuses to play the game you've suggested. You should:

(A) Sternly tell the child he must play.
(B) Wait a few minutes then suggest the same game.
(C) Send the child to bed without dinner.
(D) Ask the child what he would prefer to play.

Redirect Behavior

Provide a child with an alternate, approved activity. For example, if a child is throwing toys indoors, suggest that you go outside and play catch. If a child begins to draw on the wall, give him a piece of paper to draw on instead.

Tell Children What You Want Them to Do

Instead of "Don't run," tell children, "Walk please." "Roll the ball on the floor" tells a child what he should do instead of throwing. "Talk quietly" helps a child to know you want him to lower his voice.

Consequences

Sometimes children need to know that their misbehavior has consequences. The consequence should relate to the behavior. Ask parents about appropriate ways to handle these situations. If a child is throwing blocks, tell him, "Blocks are for building. Please build with them on the floor." If the child continues to throw the blocks, a consequence may be needed. For example, you could put the blocks away and help him find another activity.

What Should You Do?

The 6-year-old you put to bed an hour ago keeps getting up. You should:

A Let her watch TV until she goes to sleep.
B Scold the child and give her a time out.
C Call the child's parents and ask them what to do.
D Calmly return her to bed.

Babysitter's Checklist

Babysitting may seem like an overwhelming job. There's a lot to learn and a lot to remember. Keep the most important things in mind and you'll be prepared and ready to go.

Before You Begin ...

- ❏ Discuss your plans with your parents or guardians. Talk about how often and for whom you will be babysitting. Figure out how babysitting will fit into your schedule.
- ❏ Take babysitting training and first-aid courses.
- ❏ Interview any families you might be working for. Decide if the family is a good fit.
- ❏ Determine how much you will charge and how you will manage your money.

When You Arrive ...

❑ Find out where the parents are going and when they will return home. Confirm how to contact them in an emergency.

❑ Find out if you need to feed, bathe, or perform any other routines with the children. Discuss with parents the best process for performing these activities.

❑ Find out if the children are having any special issues you should know about.

❑ Be sure you know where emergency supplies are kept and how to use them.

❑ Be sure you know what to do if a stranger comes to the door or calls on the phone.

While You Are There ...

❑ Pay attention!

❑ Never leave children alone.

❑ Keep children away from unsafe objects or parts of the home.

❑ Don't play on your phone or do other activities while babysitting.

❑ Have fun and enjoy your time with the children.

No RUNNING in the HOUSE

Safety Tips Every BABYSITTER Needs to Know

The Most Important Job

Can you name a babysitter's most important job? Is it keeping the house clean or making sure the kids have a good time? That's only part of the job. A babysitter's most important job is keeping the children and herself safe.

To become the safest babysitter on the block, you'll need to enroll in safety training courses. In these classes you'll learn how to avoid dangerous situations and how to stay safe during many common babysitting activities.

What Should You Do?

You only have one week to prepare for your first babysitting job. You should spend that time ...

A learning the basics of child care and safety.

B collecting art supplies for crafts.

C learning a new recipe to cook for the children.

D deciding what to do with your first paycheck.

Before You Begin

Before you start caring for children, ask a parent or trusted adult to help you enroll in basic babysitting and safety courses. You can find these training courses through your local Red Cross, 4-H, or YMCA. You can also look for them through your school, church, community center, or scout group. If you can't find one near you, ask a parent to help you find one online.

The first class you should take is a basic first aid course. This class will teach you basic first-aid skills. These include how to help someone who is choking or how to properly care for a cut or bruise. You will learn when to call for emergency help and when to handle things yourself. In some classes you may learn how to provide CPR (cardiopulmonary resuscitation) in case a child becomes unconscious and stops breathing.

You should also take a general babysitter training course. You'll learn basic child care such as how to change a diaper and how to properly hold an infant.

Safety First

How can you be a safe babysitter before you've even accepted your first babysitting job? It's easy! Only accept jobs that you feel prepared to handle safely.

Getting to Know Each Other

Before you babysit for a new family, you should schedule an interview. In this short meeting, you can ask questions and get to know the family. Ask about the ages and number of children they want you to care for. It's also a chance for you to decide if you can safely care for the children. During the interview be sure you find out if:

- you'll be cooking any meals or bathing the children
- any of the children have special medical or physical needs
- you need to give any medications to children
- there is anything else you need to know to keep children safe

If any of the family's answers make you feel uncomfortable or overwhelmed, politely turn down the job.

Caring for Children with Physical or Medical Needs

Some children have special physical or medical needs. Before babysitting for a new family, ask the parents if their children have any conditions you should know about. You should be aware of any illnesses, allergies, or disabilities.

Remember, you're not a doctor. You don't need to know how to do everything. If a child requires medicine or special help, ask the parents to show you what to do. The ability to handle small medical issues is important. When parents know you're prepared, they'll feel more comfortable leaving their children in your care.

Allergy Alert!

Some children have allergies. Their bodies react in a negative way when they come in contact with something they are allergic to. Some children have minor allergies that cause a runny nose, itchy eyes, or a skin rash. Other children have serious allergic reactions that could lead to death. If parents tell you their child has an allergy, be sure to ask these questions:

- What is your child allergic to?
- How do I know if your child is having an allergic reaction?
- What should I do if your child has an allergic reaction?

Always Be Prepared

Make sure you arrive at each babysitting job a few minutes early. The extra time will give you a chance to go over some important information with the parents. Before parents leave, be sure you can answer all of these questions:

- Where are the parents going?
- When will the parents be home?
- At what phone number can the parents be reached?
- Who should you call in case of an emergency? What is the phone number or where is it written down?
- What is the address of the home where you are babysitting?
- Are the children having any issues you should know about?

Parents may have written down this information before you arrive. If not be sure you have recorded it in a safe place. Having this information will help you in case of an emergency.

What Should You Do?

You are babysitting a child who is playing a card game. Your friend texts you to ask what you are doing. You should ...

A continue to play the game while texting your friend back. You can multitask!

B go into another room and call her to talk.

C text her back your weekend plans. The child is playing a safe game.

D ignore her texts. You will respond to her later.

Time for a Tour!

When you arrive at a new babysitting job, ask the parents for a home tour. Ask them to show you how to lock the doors and windows and where the fire extinguishers are located. If you will be cooking, ask the parents to show you around the kitchen. If you need to give the children medications, have the parents write down instructions. Make sure you know where the medications are kept. Ask the parents to show you where their home phone is and how to use it.

If the children are allowed outdoors, ask parents if they have any special rules or areas the children should stay within. If the children go to a neighborhood park, ask the parents to write out clear directions. If the home has an alarm system, ask the parents to show you how to use it. Finally, make sure you know where the house keys are kept. That way you can lock the doors and take the keys with you if you take the children to a park.

Ask the parents to show you where each
fire extinguisher is located and how to use it.

Fire extinguisher in
lower cupboard to
the left of the sink.

The Number One Rule—Pay Attention!

It might seem like being a safe babysitter is all about following rules and keeping lists. Don't get overwhelmed. There is one rule that will keep you and the kids you're caring for safe—pay attention! Watch the children at all times. Never leave children alone and never let yourself get distracted.

Texting, playing games or checking social media on your phone, or watching TV can be tempting. But good babysitters know that these activities are distracting. Focus your attention on the children you're caring for at all times.

When children are playing, keep them away from unsafe things, including:

- scissors or other sharp objects on a table or shelf
- cords from telephones, window blinds, lamps, or other electrical appliances
- electrical outlets without covers
- small toys or small objects that could be a choking hazard
- breakable dishes or special items on low shelves or tables

Remember, if an accident or emergency happens while you're babysitting, stay calm! Staying calm will help you figure out what action to take.

Choking Hazard

Infants and toddlers can easily choke on small objects. For children under 3, that's any toy smaller than 1.75 inches (4.5 cm) across. That's the size of this circle.

1¾ inches

4½ centimeters

Always Stay Safe

A babysitter needs to keep safety in mind at all times. Staying safe is easy when you follow safety tips for different activities.

Bath Time

Bath time might seem like a relaxing event for you, but when you're babysitting it's a time to stay on your toes.

Remember!

Children can drown in as little as 1 inch (2.5 cm) of water. Never leave a child alone around any body of water, even if it's shallow.

Babysitters usually don't have to give children a bath. If parents do ask you to bathe their children, be sure to discuss their bath-time routine. Remember, babysitters should never bathe infants.

Before you put a child in the bath, make sure the water isn't too hot. If the children are playing with bath toys, double check that they aren't too small. Young children can choke on small, hard toys. Finally, help children step in and out of the bath. You don't want them to slip and fall.

Pool Safety

What's the best way to spend a hot afternoon? Splashing in the pool, of course! If you are babysitting school-age children, you might take them to a local pool. You must have their parents' permission first. Talk with parents about safety and their children's abilities.

These pool safety tips will keep you and the children safe, happy, and cool:

- Only swim at a pool where a lifeguard is on duty. Never take children swimming in a private backyard pool.
- Don't let children run near the pool.
- Ask the parents what sunscreen or other sun protection children need. Children may need help applying sunscreen.
- Never leave the children alone at a pool—even for a minute!

It is not safe for babysitters to take infants, toddlers, or preschool age children to a swimming pool, even if a lifeguard is present. Younger children can safely cool off on a hot day by splashing around with small amounts of water. Try taking a shallow pan of water and plastic cups outside. Choose a shady area, and join the children as they splash and play.

What Should You Do?

The children you are babysitting want to go swimming, but the parents did not give you permission. You should ...

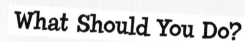

A. politely tell the children that they can go to the pool another time. Suggest a different activity.

B. ask all the children if they can swim. If they say yes, take them to the pool.

C. call the parents and ask them for permission.

D. call a friend and ask if she can help you watch the children at the pool.

Staying Safe While Playing Outdoors

Feeling cooped up indoors? It might be the right time to get outside and enjoy the sunshine. Just remember these safety tips.

- If parents have given you permission to go outdoors, take all the children outside together. Never let one or two children stay inside alone. If one child needs to go inside to use the bathroom, take all the children inside with you. Only go to play areas or parks that the parents told you about. Be sure you know how to get to the play areas so you don't get lost.

- Before going outside, remind children that you must be able to see them at all times. If you walk to a nearby park, the children must hold your hand until you arrive.

- Look around the play area to make sure it's safe. Keep children away from broken glass, pieces of metal, or other sharp objects.

- Playground equipment that is designed for older children is not safe for infants and toddlers. If playground equipment is available for very young children, use the safety straps.

- Do not allow children to play in or near a street or parking lot. If children want to roller skate, rollerblade, bike, or skateboard, make sure they wear helmets and pads. Only play in a car-free area.

Safety Straps

Always fasten the safety straps when you put a young child in a high chair, on a changing table, or in a stroller. Ask the parents if you are unsure of how to properly fasten safety straps. Always stay nearby when a child is strapped into something. Never leave a baby on a bed, sofa, or other raised area.

Staying Safe Around Strangers

You might think the only people you need to worry about while you babysit are the children. Think again. You also need to be very careful around strangers.

If you leave the house, remind children never to go anywhere with strangers or take anything from strangers. Also, never let children use public restrooms by themselves. Always go with them, and take all of the children into the restroom with you.

Even indoors you might still have to deal with strangers. Before the parents leave, ask them if they want you to answer the door or phone while they are gone. If they do, make sure to stay safe. If a stranger comes to the door, never let him or her inside. Tell the stranger the parents are busy and cannot come to the door. Never tell strangers that you are babysitting or that the parents are away. This rule applies to strangers who call on the phone too.

If you ever feel unsafe while you are babysitting, call your parents, a trusted adult, or the police.

Be a Safe Chef!

Some parents might ask you to prepare a meal for the children you are babysitting. Whether this involves the oven, microwave, or no cooking at all, you still need to stay safe. Remember these safety tips so that you don't have to swap your chef's hat for a doctor's coat!

- Get exact information about what to make from the parents and what appliances to use.
- Wash your hands before and after meal preparation.
- Keep children away from sharp tools such as knives or scissors.
- Make sure children don't touch any hot pans or cooking surfaces. When cooking on a stove, turn the handles of pans to the back of the stove.
- Cut food for younger children into very small bites. Sit at a table with the children as they eat. Encourage children to chew their food well.
- Double check that all cooking appliances are turned off after the meal.
- Clean up after the meal carefully. Wipe up any spills. Put leftover food in covered containers, and place them in the refrigerator.

Just because you're busy in the kitchen doesn't mean you can stop paying attention to the children. Give children a quiet, safe activity to do. Make sure the children play near you so you can see them. You need to be sure they are staying safe.

Wash Your Hands

When caring for children, remember to help prevent the spread of germs. Wash your hands before preparing a meal. Wash your hands and the children's hands before and after eating. Also wash your hands after diapering, helping a child use the toilet, wiping a runny nose, and whenever hands are dirty. Washing your hands will help keep you and the children from becoming ill.

What Should You Do?

You are babysitting a child who begins vomiting. You should ...

A make the child a bowl of chicken noodle soup.

B call the parents and tell them. Keep the child calm and offer him or her a small drink of water. Clean up the vomit. Then wash your hands.

C ignore it. The parents can take care of it when they get home.

D put the child in bed and clean up the vomit.

CHAPTER

3

You're HiRED!

Business Basics

Every

BABYSITTER

Needs to Know

The Business of Babysitting

Babysitting requires a lot of training and a lot of hard work. But it is also a business. After you've learned the basics of child care and safety, it's time to start learning the rules of business. Once you master the basics of starting and managing your business, your schedule could be full of babysitting jobs and your piggy bank full of spending money.

Got the Time?

Starting your own business is exciting and fun. But first make sure you will have time for it. If you are already very busy with homework, wait until the summer to open your business.

If you are involved in school activities, such as band or a sports team, remember to make time for these. Dedicate one or two days a week to these activities, and never schedule babysitting jobs on those days.

Also make sure you have your parents' permission to babysit. Discuss with them how much you plan on babysitting and if they will need to drive you to any jobs.

First Things First

Before you start any business, you'll need some training. You wouldn't open a bakery without learning how to bake cookies. And you wouldn't want to start babysitting without the needed child care, safety, and business skills. Be sure you have taken basic safety and babysitting training courses. Parents will want you to have this important information before leaving their children in your care. The more training you have, the more likely you are to get hired.

In addition to learning important child care and safety skills, a babysitting training course will also teach you how to be a smart businessperson. You'll learn about organizing your schedule, acting professionally, and building a strong business.

Getting Experience

Some parents may want you to have babysitting experience before they hire you. If you've never babysat before, don't worry. Ask neighbors or family friends about volunteer babysitting for them while they're home. If you are nervous, ask one or both parents to stay in the same room with you and the children. As you get more comfortable, they can relax in other parts of the house while you care for their children. This is a great way to learn about and gain babysitting experience. You can ask the parents for any help or advice you need. The parents will enjoy the free child care too!

What Should You Do?

You are interested in learning how to care for babies. You hear from your friends at school that your neighbors have a newborn. What should you do?

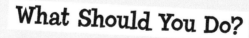

A Ask your neighbors if you can come over and help them care for the baby free of charge while they are home.

B Take a class on infant care.

C Ask a trusted adult for tips on caring for babies.

D All of the above.

Be a Business Pro

Once you've learned how to safely care for children, it's time to think about how you'll run your babysitting business.

Money Matters

One of the first things to decide is your rate, or how much money you will charge per hour. Ask friends who babysit about their rates. Do they charge extra for more than one child? Do they charge more to work on the weekends or late at night? If so, how much? Also ask your parents, neighbors, or other trusted adults with children how much they pay their babysitters. Try to set a rate that is comparable to what your friends and other babysitters charge.

Some customers might want to pay a flat rate. This means they will pay you the same amount for every babysitting job. Make sure you discuss this with them before accepting a job.

Once you have decided on your rate, stick with it. Try not to charge different customers different rates. It will be confusing, and some customers might be upset if they learn they are paying more than others.

Discuss with customers ahead of time if they will be paying you with cash or a check. If you don't already have a bank account, you may want to ask a parent to help you get one started.

Track Your Earnings

Keep your finances organized. A good way to do this is to keep a money log on your computer or in a notebook. After each job write down the date you babysat, who you worked for, how much you charged per hour, and if you got a tip.

Date	Family	Rate per hour	Number of hours	Tip
Nov. 3	Johnsons	$8	5	$5
Dec. 5	Patels	Flat fee: $30	3	none

Earning Money

What will you do with all the money you make? It's a good idea to plan how you will spend your money. Try making a pie chart showing the percentages you hope to save, spend, and put back into your business.

30%
spending money

5%
babysitting supplies

65%
savings

What Should You Do?

You agree to babysit one child and explain your single-child rate. But when you arrive, the parents tell you you'll be watching three children instead of one. What should you do?

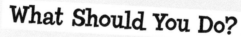

A Tell them you agreed to babysit one child, not three. Go back home.

B Agree but explain that you will need to charge extra for the other children. You will also need to confirm that the other children's parents know that you are babysitting.

C Say nothing about the additional children. You don't want to be rude.

D Tell them you will stay only if the other children leave.

Become a Master of Marketing

All successful businesses need customers. You might already have a few customers. But you can take your business to the next level with some simple marketing.

A great way to market yourself is to make flyers and business cards. These are like small advertisements for your business. Make colorful flyers and hand them out to your neighbors, teachers, and family friends. Make sure to include your rate, qualifications, and the training courses you have taken. Also include the times you are available to work.

Do you have friends who regularly babysit? Ask if you can contact their customers about being a backup babysitter when your friends are unavailable.

Remember!

Always be safe. Never give anything with your contact information to strangers. Never post your flyers in public places.

Bella's Babysitting Business

QUALIFICATIONS:
Red Cross certified
Babysitter Training Course certified
First Aid certified

AVAILABILITY:
Monday through Thursday,
4:00 p.m.–8:00 p.m.

RATE:
$8 per hour for one child
plus $1 per hour for every additional child

Contact Information: 555-8910
BellaBabysits@teenemail.com

Bella's
Babysitting Business

Monday–Thursday
4:00 p.m.–8:00 p.m.

$8 per hour for one child
plus $1 per hour for every additional child

Business Cards

Business cards are small pieces of paper that tell people your name, your business, and how you can be reached. They don't contain as much information as a flyer, but they are easy to carry in your pocket or wallet.

To make your own business cards, cut thick paper into small rectangles. Then write your business name on one side and your name and contact information on the other side. Keep five to 10 business cards with you at all times. You never know when a neighbor or family friend will be looking for a new babysitter.

Get References

References are people who can recommend you as a babysitter to others. When you work for a family, ask the parents if they would be a reference for you.

Make a Résumé

A résumé is an important tool for any businessperson. It is a short summary of you, your experience, and your interests. You can give your résumé to people you hope to babysit for.

Use this template to create your own résumé!

Your Name

your address
city, state
zip code

your phone number
your e-mail address

Education

your school

your grade level

Training

any courses you have taken and a brief description of each

Babysitting Experience

family name   date
brief description of your babysitting duties

family name   date
brief description of your babysitting duties

Hobbies

any hobbies or special interests you have

References

name   phone number   relationship to you
name   phone number   relationship to you

The Right Customers

When a parent or guardian responds to your flyer, arrange to meet him or her for an interview. This is a short meeting where you can ask questions and get to know the family. Ask a trusted adult or older sibling to go with you.

Be Choosy

Just as customers choose their babysitters, you can choose your customers. Make sure that you feel comfortable with the family during your interview. Does the family have a newborn, a child with special needs, or more children than you can comfortably care for? Think about what you're ready and able to handle. If you feel uncomfortable with the parents or children, don't take any babysitting jobs from the family.

If the customer doesn't live close to you, talk about how you will get to and from their home. Make sure you have a safe and reliable ride for every babysitting job you accept. If you live close enough to walk, always ask a trusted adult to walk with you.

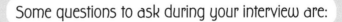

Some questions to ask during your interview are:

- How many children do you have? How old are they?
- Do any of your children have special needs or illnesses?
- What days and times will you need a babysitter?
- Do you have pets? If so, is the babysitter expected to care for them?
- Will you need a babysitter on a regular basis or just for special occasions?

Making the Right Impression

It's important to make a good impression during your interview. Do your best to show that you are a great babysitter who is responsible and caring. Wear clean and appropriate clothing. And remember to bring your résumé! The family will want to ask you questions too. Be prepared to answer these or similar questions.

- How long have you been a babysitter?
- How many families do you babysit for?
- What is your favorite thing about babysitting?
- What types of activities would you do with my children?
- Have you ever had an emergency while babysitting? If so, what did you do?

What Should You Do?

You get an e-mail from someone who says they saw one of your babysitting flyers. They want you to babysit right now. You've never met them, but they offer you more than twice your rate. What should you do?

A Tell the customer that before you work for a stranger, you always arrange a meeting that includes your parent or other trusted adult. Ask if they would like to arrange a meeting.

B Go ahead! It's going to be a big payday!

C Agree to the job, but tell a friend where you're going before you leave.

D Call the police. This sounds dangerous.

Grow Your Business

The best way to get new customers is to do a great job for the families you already work for. When you impress parents with your child care skills and professionalism, they are more likely to recommend you to others.

Being Professional

Always try to do your very best when you babysit. Treat every job as though it is the most important babysitting job ever. Acting in a professional manner shows that you take your job seriously. Here are some professional practices to follow:

- Before you accept a job, make sure you're available. Also get your parents' permission.
- Let the family know if you have a curfew.
- Only cancel a babysitting job if there is an emergency or you are sick. Let the family know as soon as possible.
- Arrive on time and be ready to work.
- Follow the parents' instructions and house rules.
- Clean up after yourself and any messes the children make while under your care.
- Do not use your cell phone, smoke, use drugs or alcohol, invite friends over, or look through the family's belongings.

Babysit for a Group

After you have gotten comfortable babysitting for one family at a time, you can grow your business by babysitting for more than one family at once. Look for chances to provide child care at neighborhood picnics, church gatherings, or parties. These events are a great way to meet new families and show them your babysitting skills. Remember, never accept a babysitting job that you are not comfortable with. Always make sure you can do a good job caring for every single child.

Tips for Babysitting a Group

- ❏ Only agree to babysit as many children as you are comfortable with.
- ❏ Only volunteer to babysit a group of children if parents are nearby.
- ❏ Ask parents if any of the children are having any issues you should know about. Know whom to contact in an emergency.
- ❏ Be sure you are in a place where you can see all children at all times. Don't ever leave children alone.
- ❏ Plan an activity or game to keep the children occupied. Bring a book and have story time. You're more likely to be able to keep control of the children if you have their attention.

Keeping It Straight

Once word gets out about your amazing babysitting business, you can expect to hear from more families. It's important to stay organized so that you know when you have booked jobs and when you are available to work. Create a calendar to help you keep everything straight.

Use a calendar to organize your schedule. You can set an alert on your phone or computer, or hang a paper calendar in your room.

Include the following details for each job in your calendar:

- family's address and phone number
- name of family and names and ages of their children
- work hours
- how you will get there and back

Monday **March 30**	study for history test

Tuesday **March 31**	Babysit at the Schneiders • 34 Oaklane Dr. • 555-5309 Children: Suzette (age 5), Dylan (age 2), and Nolan (6 months) Time: 4:00–7:00 p.m. Transportation: Mr. Schneider will pick me up and drop me off

Wednesday **April 1**	practice for violin recital

Thursday **April 2**	Babysit at the Dells • 9867 Main Ave. • 555-8910 Children: Matilda (age 10) and John (age 4) Time: 5:00–7:30 p.m. Transportation: Mom will drive me there and back

Friday **April 3**	sleepover at Stella's

Saturday **April 4**	Babysit at the Changs • 5412 Waverly Pl. • 555-7902 Children: Allison (age 7) and Chloe (age 4) Time: 1:00–4:00 p.m. Transportation: I will ride my bike

Sunday **April 5**	family movie day

Remember!

Send thank-you notes to families after you babysit for them for the first time. This tells them that you enjoyed spending time with their children. It will also let them know that you are interested in working for them in the future.

Take Care of Yourself

Have fun. Babysitting is a job, but you should enjoy it. Try not to take on too many babysitting jobs. Save some time for yourself. If you work too often, you might find yourself falling behind on homework, feeling stressed, or missing your friends.

What Should You Do?

You've got a big violin recital in two days, and you need to practice. A neighbor calls and asks if you can babysit tomorrow night for three hours. What should you do?

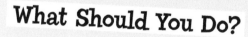

A Accept the job. You can practice after you get home from babysitting, even if it makes you tired.

B Accept the job and plan to bring your violin. You can practice while the kids play.

C Politely turn the job down. You need to practice the violin and rest before the recital.

D Tell the neighbor you'll think about it and quickly hang up the phone. You don't have time for this!

Babysitting Briefcase

You might have seen an adult carrying a briefcase to work. Why not make your own babysitting briefcase to bring along with you on your jobs? Find an old backpack or bag and fill it with items such as these:

- babysitting journal—write down any special notes about the children you babysit, such as favorite foods and bedtime rules so you will be prepared for future jobs
- your planner or calendar
- small bills in case your customers need you to make change
- homework or a book to read after the kids go to bed
- crafts or activities to do with the children

Let's **PLAY!**

Awesome Activities
Every
BABYSITTER
Needs to Know

Play Is Fun and Important

Watching someone's children is a big responsibility. Babysitting is a business you need to take seriously. But that doesn't mean it can't be fun. In fact, play is good for you and for the children you babysit.

Why Play Is Good

Happy and busy children are more likely to behave, which will make your job easier. When the children you babysit are happy and behaving, you know you're doing a good job. Families will hire you again and refer you to other families.

Different Ways to Play

Play is important for a child's growth and learning. There are different types of play. Each type helps children in meaningful ways.

- Active play, such as running, jumping, swinging, and dancing, helps children develop physically.
- Creative play, such as drawing, painting, making music, and make-believe, helps children use their imaginations.
- Thinking games, such as sorting, solving puzzles, counting, and learning rhymes, improve children's minds.
- Social play, such as team sports or taking turns on the playground, helps children learn to get along with others.
- Quiet play, such as reading or looking at books, playing with small table toys, or coloring, helps children calm down.

Doing activities with the children you babysit is a win for everyone. But before you set up that board game or twirl a jump rope, there are a few things you need to know.

Before You Play

There are several things to keep in mind when planning activities. Safety always comes first. You should also know what parents will allow. Choose activities that are appropriate for the child's age. Being flexible and planning ahead will help you and the children stay safe and have fun.

What Should You Do?

The girl you're babysitting falls while riding her bike. She's crying. You should first ...

A call 9-1-1.
B check to make sure you and the child are in a safe place.
C promise her a snack if she'll stop crying.
D laugh at her for being clumsy.

Play Safely

Here are some tips for keeping everyone safe and happy during play:

- Play with the children. Don't just watch. It's not OK for you to start them on an activity and then go watch TV, do homework, or text your friends. Joining in gives you a chance to model good behavior. It may also help prevent behavior problems before they start.
- Read all toy and game warnings and directions. Know how toys work and how to use them. Check the ages recommended on the box or instructions. Only use toys or games that are appropriate for the child's age.
- Make sure children under age 3 don't have access to objects they could swallow or choke on. If an object can fit through a cardboard paper towel tube, it's a choking hazard.
- Put all risky toys out of reach of infants and toddlers. These include toys with tears, loose buttons, broken parts, sharp points, long strings, and electronic toys that might cause burns.
- Wash your hands before and after playing.

Follow House Rules

Every family is different. One family may think it's fine for children to tap dance on the hardwood floors. Another family may frown on dancing entirely. If a parent doesn't tell you the rules up front, ask what they are. Here are some questions to ask when planning activities:

TV and Video Games: Can the children watch TV or play video games? Is there a time limit? Are there any programs, channels, or games that are off limits? How late can they watch or play?

Computers and Phones: Are the children allowed to use computers, tablet devices, or the phone? If so, what activities are allowed and for how long?

Going Outside: Can you take the children outside? If so, do they need to stay in the yard, or can you take them for a walk? If so, how far are you allowed to go?

Active Play: Are children allowed to be rowdy and run around? Or do parents want them to play calmly and quietly?

You may have a special activity in mind that's not covered by any of these house rules. Always get a parent's permission first.

Choose Appropriate Activities

As children grow, their interests and abilities change. For example, a 1-year-old boy is too young to play Monopoly. And his 10-year-old brother doesn't want to play peek-a-boo. Choosing the right activities for the age of the child helps keep everyone safe. Age-appropriate activities that interest the child help prevent behavior problems by keeping him or her from becoming frustrated or bored.

What Should You Do?

You've started a craft. The girl you're babysitting yells, "This is stupid!" and walks away. You should ...

A ask the child what she would like to play.

B continue the craft on your own, hoping the child will see how much fun you're having.

C scold the child for being rude.

D give up doing any activities and go watch TV.

Be Flexible

Not all children enjoy the same things. Some children are more active than others. If a child doesn't want to play a certain game or activity, respect his or her wishes. Ask the child what he or she would like to play. Children also mature differently and reach stages of development at different times. If you're unsure about a child's abilities, ask parents what kinds of activities their child enjoys.

Plan Ahead

You will be babysitting two school-age children and have an amazing craft project in mind. Plan ahead by making a list of all the supplies you'll need. Does the family have these supplies? If not, who will buy them—you or the parents? If you provide the materials, do you expect to be repaid? Work out these details with a parent ahead of time.

Plan for how long a game or project will take. Will the parents only be gone an hour? Are the children going to bed soon? If so, don't start a craft or game that will take two hours. Also consider time to prepare and cleanup.

If you're babysitting more than one child, plan how you'll keep everyone occupied, especially if the children are different ages. If you do a single activity, be sure it is safe and appropriate for all children. Multiple activities are OK as long as you can safely watch every child at once. Be wise. Don't take on more than you or the kids can handle.

Clean Up After the Fun

When you're finished playing, return all toys and games where you found them. Put game pieces back neatly inside their boxes. The house should look as clean when you leave as it did when you arrived. Children can help you with cleaning up.

Activity Ideas for Infants and Toddlers

You have an awesome idea for an activity and it meets parents' approval. It's age appropriate and safe. Now it's time to play. Use your creativity and imagination.

Here are some examples of age-appropriate toys, games, and activities if you're running low on ideas.

Activities for Young Infants (Newborn to 6 Months)

Babies like to play on their own rather than with other children. They may only stay interested in an activity for a few minutes. So be patient and don't expect too much. Here are some toys and activities young infants may enjoy:

- simple toys with bright colors
- stuffed animals without buttons that could be a choking hazard
- teething toys
- rattles
- being held and rocked
- being cooed and sung to
- cloth or board books

Things to See and Hear

Babies like having different things to look at and listen to. Move the infant from one spot to another, giving him or her different things to look at. Even shadows from a window or the movement of a ceiling fan can be interesting to an infant. Talk, coo, or sing to the infant often. If it's a nice day, take the baby for a walk.

107

Activities for Older Infants
(6 Months to 1 Year)

Lots of development takes place between the ages of 6 months and 1 year. At 6 months babies are supporting their own heads. Soon after they're sitting, rolling, scooting, and crawling. At 9 to 12 months, babies are standing and some are taking their first steps. They may act shy with new people, but they like to watch and imitate others. Toys and activities older infants may enjoy include:

- large, soft blocks
- big stacking boxes or cups
- teething toys
- things that make noise, such as pots and pans, large bells, and squeaky toys
- throwing or dropping nonbreakable objects
- rolling a ball
- cloth books and simple picture books
- games like patty cake and peek-a-boo

Box of Fabric

Infants like to look and touch. Fill a small box with large squares of fabric of different colors and textures. Include fabrics that are soft, rough, silky, shiny, light, and dark. Pull a piece of fabric from the box and describe how it feels. Then give it to the baby to touch. Say, "This fabric feels soft. Would you like to touch the soft fabric?"

Activities for Toddlers
(1 to 3 Years)

Toddlers love to learn and do things for themselves. They also like to move around. What they don't love is to share, which means they don't make the best playmates. But they will play on their own beside other children. Some fun toys and activities for toddlers include:

- push and pull toys, like a toy wagon or shopping cart
- musical toys, like drums and shakers
- riding toys
- moving toys, like planes, cars, and trucks
- washable crayons, markers, and play dough
- toys that need arranging, like shape sorters and rings
- blocks for stacking and lining up to make roads
- dancing, rolling, jumping, and running
- singing songs
- imitating grown-ups and playing simple dress-up
- looking at picture books and being read to

Things in a Can

Toddlers can usually be entertained with simple games. Try cutting a hole in the lid of a large plastic tub. Make sure there are no sharp edges. Put the lid back on the container. Let the toddler drop craft sticks, clothespins, spoons, or other nonbreakable items inside. Be sure none of the objects are small enough to choke on. When finished, let the toddler dump the items out.

Activity Ideas for Preschoolers and School-Age Children

By age 3 children are becoming more coordinated. They can focus for longer periods of time and do more for themselves. The older the children are, the more creative you can be with your activities.

Activities for Preschoolers (3 to 5 Years)

Children between the ages of 3 and 5 start to interact with each other. They like to play simple games, but they may want to make up their own rules. Some toy and play ideas for preschoolers include:

- easy board games such as Chutes and Ladders and Candy Land
- pretend games such as playing school and shopping
- draping a sheet or blanket over a table or two chairs to make a tent
- stories read aloud
- jigsaw puzzles with big pieces
- hide-and-seek or tag
- riding wagons or tricycles
- playing musical instruments, such as drums, kazoos, or toy guitars
- playing with play dough or clay
- going on a treasure hunt
- making crafts, such as bookmarks, brown lunch bag puppets, collages, or necklaces made from cereal Os or dry macaroni

Treasure Hunt

A treasure hunt will challenge children and be fun at the same time. Make a map of the children's backyard. Hide a "treasure" somewhere in the yard. Mark an X on the map. The X can be the location of the treasure or another clue. The clue might read, "Walk 10 steps toward the fence. Hop 5 times and squawk like a chicken. Crawl under the slide. Climb over the rock. Look behind the tree trunk." Hide as many clues as you like.

Activities for School-Age Children (5 to 10 Years)

Rules are important to children who are ages 5 to 10. They understand teamwork, taking on roles, and having a leader. The activity ideas are endless for school-age children. Keep in mind that the abilities and attention span of a 5-year-old will be less than those of a 10-year-old. Here are a few game and play ideas:

- reading books
- drawing
- action dolls and fashion dolls
- board games such as checkers, Monopoly, Clue, and Sorry
- word games such as Scrabble and Boggle
- jigsaw puzzles
- putting on a play, puppet show, or talent show
- writing a story together
- outdoor activities, such as soccer, basketball, hopscotch, jump rope, riding bikes or scooters, or throwing a football, softball, or Frisbee
- making crafts with beads, yarn, paper, paint, clay, boxes, or other materials

Puppet Show

A puppet show is a fun activity that will let children be creative. Have the children help you write a script. Decorate socks or paper bags to create a puppet for each character. Use a tabletop or cardboard box as a stage. Practice your puppet voices. Put on a final performance for parents when they get home.

What Should You Do?

You're playing a board game and two brothers start fighting. You should ...

A punish the child who started the fight.

B get up and walk away.

C sit patiently and wait for the siblings to work out their own problems.

D stop playing and talk with the children.

What Should You Do?

You're stacking blocks with a 2-year-old. Her 5-year-old sister is jealous and wants your attention. You should ...

A play with the child who is the loudest.
B play with whichever child you like the best.
C tell the 5-year-old to wait her turn.
D try to give both children equal attention.

Activities for Different Age Groups

You're babysitting an infant, a 2-year-old, and an 8-year-old. You want an activity that's fun and appropriate for all three children. Here are a few ideas for all age groups:

- Walk around the neighborhood. Take a trip to the playground or a field trip to the library.
- Roll, bounce, or throw balls into a box or laundry basket.
- Play with blocks. Infants and toddlers can stack and knock them over. Preschool and school-age children can build more detailed structures. Remember to check the size of the blocks to make sure they are safe for use by infants and toddlers.
- Make homemade musical instruments and have a parade.
- Read aloud from a book. Young children may lose interest quickly if you aren't reading a book with pictures. Give younger children board books to look at as you read to older children.

Homemade Musical Instruments

There are lots of ways to make musical instruments with the kids you're babysitting. Partially fill empty plastic spice jars with beans, buttons, or beads. Glue on the lids to make a rattle. Turn a plastic tub or coffee can upside down to make a drum. Use a wooden spoon for a drumstick. Use two saucepan lids about the same size for banging cymbals. Make a guitar by cutting a hole in a shoebox lid. Tape the lid on the shoebox, stretch a few rubber bands across the hole, and strum the rubber band "strings."

Activities Tote Kit

It's a good idea to keep supplies ready so you can grab them on your way to any babysitting job. Keep items together in one place. A plastic box with a handle that securely fastens is a good choice. If you don't plan on being reimbursed for your supplies, don't spend too much money. The supplies should last through several babysitting jobs.

Some things you might want to include are:

- drawing paper (you can store paper items in folders or envelopes)
- crayons
- colored pencils
- sidewalk chalk
- glue stick
- old magazines for making collages
- safety scissors to use with preschool and school-age children
- play dough or other non-hardening clay stored in an airtight container
- blowing bubbles
- hand puppets
- a list of age-appropriate games and activities
- activity how-to descriptions

Be a Great Babysitter!

Babysitting may seem like a huge job. And it is. It takes a responsible and knowledgeable person to be a great babysitter. Do you have what it takes? Remembering these basic rules of the trade will keep you and the kids you're caring for happy and safe.

Get trained. Before you begin babysitting, make sure you have the proper child care and safety skills. If you're babysitting for other families, know how much you will charge and how you will manage your money.

Communicate with the parents of the children you're babysitting. Always know where parents are going and how to contact them. Know their expectations for you and what their rules are. Be aware of any issues their children may have.

Pay attention. Be alert, and be aware of your surroundings. Never leave a child unattended. This will help prevent negative behavior and dangerous situations.

Be prepared for anything to happen. If there's an emergency or a child can't seem to behave, stay calm. Take a deep breath and use your babysitting know-how to figure out the best way to handle the situation.

Have fun. Plan ahead of time how you will occupy the children you are babysitting. The hours will fly by, and the kids won't be able to wait for you to come back.

What Should You Do?
Quiz Answers

page 15

C Decline the sleepover invitation and go to your babysitting job.

Stay professional and keep your commitments.

page 23

B Stay with the child and do not answer the door.

Never leave a young child alone. If there is an emergency and you must leave the bedroom, finish dressing the child and take him with you.

page 29

D Ask the child what he would prefer to play.

Be flexible. Never force a child to do an activity he doesn't want to do. Suggest an alternative activity. Or ask the child what he would like to do. It could also be that the child is tired, hungry, or not feeling well. Try to find out.

page 31

D Calmly return the child to bed.

Be kind, but firmly stick to the child's normal sleep routine. Try reading a story, playing an imaginary game, or listening to soft music.

page 37

A learning the basics of child care and safety.

Take a first aid or babysitting class if you can. Before you babysit, you need to know how to safely care for children. You'll also learn how to act in an emergency.

page 45

D ignore her texts. You will respond to her later.

Never text or call your friends while you are babysitting. The children you are caring for need your full attention!

page 53

A politely tell the children that they can go to the pool another time. Suggest a different activity.

Only take children swimming (or on other outings) if their parents have clearly given you permission. Make sure to discuss safety rules with their parents too.

page 61

B call the parents and tell them. Keep the child calm and offer her a small drink of water. Clean up the vomit. Then wash your hands.

Whenever a child you babysit becomes ill, call and tell the parents. They might have special instructions for you to follow. If a child has vomited, clean her up. Then offer her very small sips of water. Stay with her until the parents return home.

page 69

D All of the above.

Make sure you know how to feed, diaper, and care for infants before you babysit one. Ask an adult for tips and take a babysitting course if you can. Volunteer babysitting an infant is also a great way to learn about baby care.

page 73

B Agree, but explain that you will need to charge extra for the other children. You will also need to confirm that the other children's parents know that you are babysitting.

Babysitting more than one child is more work. Be sure you get paid for your work. Call the parents of the other children to confirm they know you are babysitting. Be sure to ask if their children have any special issues you need to be aware of.

page 81

A Tell the customer that before you work for a stranger, you always arrange a meeting that includes your parent or other trusted adult. Ask if they would like to arrange a meeting.

Never accept a job from a stranger without first scheduling an interview. Make sure that each babysitting job you accept is safe.

page 89

C Politely turn the job down. You need to practice the violin and rest before the recital.

Your babysitting jobs should not take away from your homework or extracurricular activities. You also shouldn't schedule so many babysitting jobs that you don't have any time for yourself.

page 98

B check to make sure you and the child are in a safe place.

After making sure you're both safe, speak calmly and reassuringly to the child. Find out if the child is hurt or just scared. If the child has an injury you can take care of yourself, like a scraped knee, then follow proper first-aid procedures. Call 911 if the injury is life threatening. Then call the child's parents. Only do what you're trained to do.

page 102

A ask the child what she would like to play.

Be flexible. You might also want to dig deeper, and find out why the child doesn't want to play.

page 115

D stop playing and talk with the children.

It doesn't matter who started the fight. Let the children know that fighting is not allowed. Ask the children if they need help working things out. Decide whether it's best to continue the game or do something else.

page 116

D try to give both children equal attention.

You are a special person in the children's house. Both children will want your attention. Ask the 5-year-old to help you stack blocks with the 2-year-old.

Bonus Questions!

Now that you've reviewed the babysitting basics, it's time to test your knowledge. What would you do in the following situations?

The preschooler you're babysitting starts to hit his sister. You should first:

A Calmly separate the children.
B Yell at him to stop.
C Do nothing. Let them work it out themselves.
D Yank the preschooler by the arm and send him to his room.

A First, separate the children. If the other child has been hurt, comfort her and take care of any injuries she may have. Then react calmly to the child who has done the hitting. Tell him it's not OK to hurt someone else when he's angry.

A 5-year-old starts throwing her toy blocks around the room. You should:

A Take her toys away.
B Talk to her about her behavior then redirect her to a more acceptable activity.
C Put her in a time-out until she calms down.
D Punish her by taking away her TV privileges.

B Children don't always understand how their behavior affects others. You might say, "When you throw your blocks, you might hurt yourself or someone else." Then redirect her to another activity.

You are asked to cook dinner for three children. One of the kids wants to help you cook. You should ...

A suggest some ways that the child can safely help.

B tell the child to put on an apron. You don't want clothes getting dirty.

C tell the child that sounds great! Check your e-mail while the child does the work.

D have the child go play in another room. You don't want anyone in the way.

A Depending on the child's age, think of ways the child can safely help as you prepare a meal. Toddlers can help set the table and help you wash fruit and vegetables. Older children can pour milk into cups, tear lettuce to make a salad, and take bowls of cold food to the table. Make sure you can see the child while you are busy cooking.

You have taken the children to a nearby park for the afternoon. One of the children has to go to the bathroom. You should ...

A take all the children to the bathroom together. Stay with the children.

B let the child to go to the bathroom alone. Tell her to hurry.

C tell the child to wait until you can get home.

D take the child to the bathroom. Tell the other children not to move until you get back.

A Never leave children alone. If one child has to go to the bathroom, take all the children with you. Always go with children into public restrooms.

Index

Credits

Capstone Young Readers are published by Capstone,
1710 Roe Crest Drive, North Mankato, Minnesota 56003
www.capstoneyoungreaders.com

Library of Congress Cataloging-in-Publication Data
Higgins, Melissa, 1953-
   Babysitter's backpack : everything you need to be a safe, smart, and skilled babysitter / by Melissa Higgins and Rebecca Rissman.
       pages cm
   Includes index.
   ISBN 978-1-62370-134-5 (paperback)
   Summary: "From safety to childcare basics to managing your own business, get the skills you need to become a great babysitter"—Provided by publisher.
   1. Babysitting—Handbooks, manuals, etc.—Juvenile literature. 2. Babysitters—Handbooks, manuals, etc.—Juvenile literature. [1. Babysitting—Handbooks, manuals, etc.] I. Rissman, Rebecca. II. Title.
   HQ769.5.H5394 2015
   649'.10248—dc23

                    2014022144

Editorial Credits
Abby Colich, editor; Juliette Peters, designer;
Tracy Cummins, media researcher; Katy LaVigne, production specialist

Content Consultant
Lyn Horning, Assistant Director, Better Kid Care,
Penn State University, University Park, Pennsylvania

Photo Credits
Alamy: © Catchlight Visual Services, 6 (middle left), 18, 21, David Young-Wolff, 108, Radius Images, 9; Capstone Studio: Karon Dubke, 2 (all), 3 (l), 6 (bottom left), 11, 13, 17, 19 (top), 22, 23 (t), 26, 27, 29 (b), 31 (t), 32, 33, 34 (ml), 36, 40, 41, 42, 43, 44, 45, 46, 48, 49 (t), 51, 56, 57, 60 (t), 62 (all l), 64, 69 (t), 70, 73 (t), 74 (t), 76 (t), 78, 80, 81 (t), 82, 83, 88 (b), 92 (t,ml), 95, 99, 101, 102 (t), 103, 104, 106, 109 (t), 111 (t), 115 (b), 117 (t); Getty Images Inc: Fuse, 58, Hero Images, 14, lostinbids, 30; iStockphotos: ©Mienny, 72, ©RusianDashinsky, 120, ©Steve Debenport, 5, ©vjajic, 15 (t), ©skynesher, 84, jo unruh, 92 (bl), 110, Kali Nine LLC, 68, metinkiyak, 98 (t), Yuri_Acurs, 97; Photoshot: ©Caro, 34 (tl), 39; Science Source: Voisin/Phanie, 55 (t); Shutterstock: Africa Studio, 119 (middle), Agorohov, 119 (right), arek_malang, cover, 90, BlueOrange Studio, 10, bogdan ionescu, 119 (l), Denis Cristo, illustrated girls in various clothes, design element, Denis Kuvaev, 94, Elena Stepanova, 75 (b), 76 (b), Ersier Dmitry, 52, forestpath, 89 (t), Golden Pixels LLC, 85, GWImages, 12, komkrit Preechachanwate, 91 (b), lightpoet, 67, Lena S, 20, Mara008, 91 (t), Martin Novak, 118, Maryna Kulchytska, 3 (right), 113, Maya Kruchankova, 61 (b), Mazzzur, 91 (m), Mila Supinskaya, 34 (bl), 54, Monkey Business Images, 38, 50, 66, Natykach Natalia, backpack, Radharani, 59, shooarts, 47 (all), Solphoto, 100, Stephanie Barbary, 65, Stephen Denness, 121, Steve Cukrov, 71, Stocklite, 107 (t), Syda Productions, 86, Tomasz Trojanowski, 105, Vadym Zaitsev, 91 (l), Valentijn Tempels, 6 (ml), 25, Veerachai Viteeman, colored grunge design, ZouZou, 96; SuperStock: Fancy Collection, 16, 24, Kwame Zikomo, 6 (tl), 8, Voisin/Phanie, 37 (t); Thinkstock: Jupiterimages, 53 (t)

Design credits: Shutterstock

Printed in Canada.
062014   008248FRF14